G000253530

THE SPIRIT OF

PORTSMOUTH
GOSPORT & SOUTHSEA

IAIN McGOWAN

HALSGROVE

First published in Great Britain in 2007

Text copyright © Iain McGowan
Image copyright © Iain McGowan unless otherwise stated

British Library Cataloguing-in-Publication Data
A CIP record for this title is available from the British Library

ISBN 978 1 84114 664 5

HALSGROVE
Halsgrove House
Ryelands Farm Industrial Estate, Bagley Green,
Wellington, Somerset TA21 9PZ
Tel: 01823 653777 Fax: 01823 216796
email: sales@halsgrove.com
website: www.halsgrove.com

Printed and bound by D'Auria Industrie Grafiche, Italy

Introduction

Portsmouth's unique island site, surrounded on three sides by sheltered waters and protected from the north by mainland Portsdown Hill, has ensured the city's place in English History. The story of Portsmouth is the story of the country's association with the sea, trade, Empire and above all, defence and the Royal Navy. For over 2000 years Portsmouth has seen departures of naval fleets and military personnel to wars in every part of the globe, its street and pub names acting as mute reminders and a celebration of past glories; its parks and waterfront still filled with carved stone memorials engraved with the names of those who never returned.

There may not be so many arrivals and departures of grey painted warships these days but Portsmouth's Continental Ferry Port is now one of the busiest in the country; the Historic Dockyard and the Spinnaker Tower have joined seaside Southsea as major tourist attractions; the University has become a major factor in the local economy and, with the arrival of several large foreign business companies into the area together with an explosion of new technological industries, the prospects of this unique island city look bright. 'Pompey' is still a strange mixture of the old and the new, sometimes attractive, sometimes down at heel, but always of interest.

Part of the 1km-long defensive Roman wall to Portchester Castle with the city approaches in the background. The walling is over 3m thick and 6m high with a series of projecting bastions for use with catapult artillery.

Portchester Castle is a spectacular feature of the harbour. It was built by the Romans in the third century AD as one of the 'Saxon Shore' forts – a coastal defence system stretching from Portsmouth to the Wash.

Evidence of the castle's grim years as a prison can be found in the numerous examples of French grafitti carved in the stonework. At one time over 9000 prisoners were held here.

The entrance to Portsmouth Harbour with Old Portsmouth and its spit to the right and Gosport 'over the water' to the left on the western shore.

Fishing boats at anchor at Camber Quay.

In 1927 the new Diocese of Portsmouth was created and the old parish church of
St Thomas chosen as the cathedral for the new bishop and people of the city.

In memory of ADMIRAL SIR BERTRAM RAMSAY killed in action 1945 who commanded the seaborne forces at Dunkirk 1940

and Normandy 1944 here are remembered also those under his command who were killed during these operations

The two lower lights of the D-Day window in the Holy Martyrs' chapel. The window was a gift from the D-Day and Normandy Fellowship in 1984 – the fortieth anniversary of the D-Day and Normandy landings.

Crowds line the beach at the harbour entrance to watch the departure of the aircraft carrier HMS *Ark Royal* sailing for the Gulf War in early 2003.

Looking south along the walkway above Point Battery. The Square Tower is on the left and the Isle of Wight coast in the distance on the right across the waters of Spithead.

A view across the recently landscaped area of Grand Parade.

Opposite page:
The colourful mural to be found on the side of the Bridge Tavern close to Camber Quay is based on Thomas Rowlandson's watercolour of Portsmouth Point and vividly conveys in caricature the atmosphere of local life in days gone by.

The classic view from Point overlooking the harbour, the re-developed
Gunwharf Quays and the rising Spinnaker Tower.

Old Portsmouth, looking along Lombard Street.

Around Old Portsmouth

HMS *Victory*.
Referred to as the most
famous ship in British
Naval History and the
oldest commissioned
warship in the world,
HMS *Victory* has been
berthed at No 2 Dry
Dock within the dockyard
since 1922 and has
for many years been the
very symbol of Portsmouth
and its naval heritage.

The naval dockyard is one of the best examples of Georgian industrial premises in the country, containing many fine brick buildings dating back to the eighteenth century and built with a solid functional elegance.

A portion of the east window of the dockyard church of St Ann reveals a stylised bird's-eye view of part of the dockyard as seen from the semaphore tower in 1945 after the ending of the Second World War. The window by Hugh Easton is a memorial to all those who worked in and sailed from Portsmouth and who lost their lives in the war.

An almost timeless scene as HMS *Warrior* (the 'Black Snake') looms out of the mist on a damp winter's morning. HMS *Warrior* was the largest and most powerful warship of her age when she was commissioned in 1861.

No 1 Dry Dock with Monitor M33 undergoing restoration work.
Behind is the aircraft carrier HMS *Invincible*. M33 is one of only two British
First World War ships to have survived the wars and ravages of time.

The remains of the Tudor warship the *Mary Rose* undergoing preservation treatment in the Mary Rose Ship Hall.

A misty early-morning view of the dockyard seen from a departing
continental ferry with the aircraft carrier HMS *Ark Royal* at anchor.

Pat Mitchell

The Treadgold Industrial Heritage Museum. Treadgolds of Portsea was
established as an ironmonger's shop and smithy in Bishop Street in 1809
by William Treadgold, evolving over the years until final closure in 1988.

Scenes at the newly-transformed Gunwharf Quays.

The Spinnaker Tower, shown here during final stages of its construction, is the new national landmark at the entrance to Portsmouth Harbour.

With the advent of rifled, breech loading, longer-range artillery and renewed suspicions of Napoleon III's military ambitions, the whole of the Portsmouth defences were re-examined in a flurry of reports submitted during the 1850s to the Government. After many enquiries the decision was taken to construct a series of detached forts along the crest of Portsdown Hill as a first line of defence against any invasion from the north.

Spitbank Fort.
Since the eastern approach of the Solent was considered to be too wide to be protected by shore batteries or a permanent barrier, four circular reinforced granite and armour-faced sea forts were constructed spaced across the water. Protecting the deep-water approach channels, the Spithead forts were built on shallow shoals and sandbanks using prepared stone and concrete ring foundations.

A view from the spit at Eastney looking over Langstone Harbour.

The Guildhall was designed by William Hill and completed in 1890.
Built as the Landport Town Hall in an Italianate style reflecting
late Victorian municipal pride, it became known as the Guildhall
after 1926 when Portsmouth became a city.

The University of Portsmouth was inaugurated in 1992, its predecessor the former Portsmouth Polytechnic growing from the Portsmouth and Gosport School of Science and Arts originally founded in 1869.

The view looking south over the inner reaches of Portsmouth Harbour from what is now the suburb of Paulsgrove. The Norman keep of Portchester Castle can be seen in the distance whilst on the left the apartments and flats mark the entrance to Port Solent Marina.

This page and opposite:
Port Solent is one of the south coast's leading leisure attractions. Featuring the third largest marina in the UK and a considerable number of up-market shops, retail outlets, bars, pubs, restaurants, with a cinema and leisure club, it has a distinctly Mediterranean atmosphere along its boardwalks.

Part of the newly-landscaped Gosport waterfront near the ferry landing stage.

Gosport's pedestrianised High Street.

Fishing is a popular recreation on the new Haslar Marina Millennium Pier opened in 2001 with its superb views across the water to Old Portsmouth.

The Royal Navy Submarine Museum occupies part of the former
submarine base of HMS *Dolphin* at Haslar.

A view across the inner reaches of the harbour from near Hardway.

The refurbished and restored crescent at Alverstoke.

High summer on Southsea beach with South Parade Pier in the background.

Southsea rock in its many colours.

Long before Southsea was to become a resort it was realised
that the area also had considerable defensive possibilities.
Under a decree by Henry VIII in 1544 and as part of a programme
to update the 'Saxon Shore' forts, Southsea Castle was built.

The architect
Thomas Ellis
Owen's Southsea.
Features of Netley
Terrace, Queen's
Terrace and
Swiss Cottage.

South Parade Pier has had a somewhat chequered history,
the present structure being the third design on the site.

Opposite: Southsea seafront souvenirs.

49

Floating apparitions at the annual Kite Festival, Southsea Common. It was only the needs of the Army keeping the common clear of speculative development during the nineteenth century that provided Southsea with this outstanding feature today.

Aspects of Southsea.

Lest we forget.
Poignant symbols of
remembrance at the
Royal Naval War Memorial
on Southsea Common.

The memorial was designed
by Sir Robert Lorimer and
unveiled in 1924 to
commemorate the 9666
Portsmouth-based sailors who
died in the First World War.
The later walled extension
with its two pavilions on the
monument's landward side
commemorates the 14,797
sailors and marines who died
in the Second World War
and who 'have no grave
but the sea'.

Portsmouth City Museums /

The D-Day Museum was opened in 1984 to commemorate D-Day 40 and extended ten years later. The museum's centrepiece is the magnificent Overlord Tapestry commissioned by Lord Dulverton as a tribute to the sacrifice and heroism of those men and women who took part in Operation Overlord. The tapestry, designed by Sandra Lawrence, is 83m long and the longest work of its kind in the world, conceived as a modern counterpart to the Bayeux Tapestry. Pictured is a scene from the tapestry showing flotillas of Royal Navy minesweepers clearing channels ahead of the main invasion force.

Part of the Memorial Garden at the Royal Marines Museum
situated in the old Eastney Barracks at the far eastern end of the
seafront. Behind is a section of the barracks' long centre block
built in the 1860s and once used as the marines' quarters.

High summer looking from Portsdown Hill
northwards over ripening fields.

Opposite page:
A late winter's afternoon looking across the waters
of Spithead to the Isle of Wight.

The tiny secluded Saxon church of St Nicholas at Boarhunt
lies in a fold of the northern slope of Portsdown Hill. Within a
short distance of the city lies deeply attractive countryside.

Butser Hill is situated within Queen Elizabeth Country Park and at 270m is one of the highest points on the South Downs. This view from near its summit looks towards the village of East Meon in the distance.

A view looking east across Farlington Marshes local nature reserve. The reserve is the largest open space in Portsmouth and a site of international importance for birds that visit and pass through to and from places as far apart as eastern Canada, Siberia and southern Africa.

The ancient chapel of St Hubert was built in the mid eleventh century probably under the direction of Godwin, Earl of Wessex and premier Earl of England.

Wickham has been
described by Pevsner
in his *Buildings
of England* as the finest
village in Hampshire
and one of the best in
the south of England.

The ruins of the Premonstratensian Abbey at Titchfield.

Looking west along the beach at Lee-on-the-Solent towards Southampton.